7 99

ELIZABETH WHITNEY CRISCI

When Kids
Bend
The
Rules

101 CREATIVE DISCIPLINE IDEAS

D1088684

ACCENT PUBLICATIONS
Colorado Springs, Colorado

Accent Publications
4050 Lee Vance View
P.O. Box 36640
Colorado Springs, Colorado 80936

Copyright © 1991 Accent Publications
Printed in the United States of America

All rights reserved. No portion of this book may be reproduced in any
form without the written permission of the publishers, with the
exception of brief excerpts in magazine reviews.

Library of Congress Catalog Card Number 91-72822
ISBN 0-89636-276-0

Fourth Printing

Contents

SECTION TWO: NOISY—NOT NAUGHTY

SECTION THREE: MORE NAUGHTY THAN NICE

Introduction

The biggest, single problem for Christian Education workers is discipline.

Children are naturally restless; they find it hard to sit still. Many find it almost impossible to accept the authority of a teacher. Well-seasoned teachers have their problems; new teachers have "double trouble" (extreme difficulty). Many quit before they ever learn the secrets, the methods, and the joys of good discipline *When Kids Bend the Rules*.

Other teachers get locked into a class and find it next-to-impossible to escape. They just endure through the class, letting the wild students get what they wish, one way or another, and the teaching time is almost wasted.

But there is a better way. A teacher can learn to keep the interest of the students—even the "double trouble" ones—to such a high degree that they never seem to want to misbehave. This book is a compilation of *"101 Creative Discipline Ideas"* for teachers of mid-week clubs, for youth meetings, for Sunday School classes, and whatever other application may work into your lives as busy, dedicated teachers (or parents!).

Keep this book handy. Read several ideas each week...so that they will be in the mind and ready to apply as needed. If one idea works wonders with an unsettled class, reuse it, but don't stay with it. Eventually, that idea will run stale and you'll need to be ready with another idea. Keep varying the discipline ideas and they will become fun, helpful instruments used of God to get His message across to the children to whom He says, "Suffer...to come unto me: for of such is the kingdom of heaven" (Matthew 19:14).

If a teacher forgets discipline, the students who come eager to learn will be impaired right along with the students who *think* they don't want to learn. I have found the worst offenders are either (1) the most needy, or (2) those who, unknowingly, really want to learn but need special attention and know no other way than misbehaving to achieve it. So...off to better classes with more learning in a happy, disciplined, learning environment.

You can turn misbehavior into something positive.

Idea # 1: STUDENT CONTRACT

Situation: *There are always some discipline problems. At the beginning of the quarter, during the first class period, have the students decide on a few fundamental rules for good behavior before any discipline problems arise.*

Solution: As the students suggest common courtesies and good behavior rules, write them on the chalkboard. Have someone copy them on a paper. Before the next class, type them, and get them copied. Give one copy to each student. Title them, "My Contract With My Teacher," and provide a line for a signature at the bottom. At the beginning of the second class, have each student sign two contracts: one to give to the teacher and one to keep and remember.

(Feel free to guide choices and rules that are not student generated.)

My Contract With My Teacher

I will listen when the teacher is talking.
I will respect other students.
I will cooperate with the teacher.
I will do my classwork the best I can.
Signed,

_____

Desired Result: The students will have a hand in determining how they should behave and will be following their own rules. This will help them obey better than hearing teacher-imposed rules. Discipline should be good most of the time.

Items Needed: First day: chalkboard, chalk, paper, pen or marker
Second day: two typed contracts for each student, pencils (one for each class member)

Idea #2: COPY, COPY ME

Situation: *The class has been well-behaved for several minutes and needs a little change of activity before going further with a lesson.*

Solution: Call out, "COPY, COPY ME!" Ask the class to stand and follow your actions. Touch your shoulders, your hips, your toes, your waist, your ears, your knees, your opposite elbows, and the top of your head. Then quickly sit down, pause for quiet, and plunge into the rest of the lesson.

Desired Result: The class will listen better because they will be relaxed and not feel over-burdened with a long period of paying attention.

Items Needed: None

Idea #3: ONE LITTLE, TWO LITTLE, THREE LITTLE WHISTLES

Situation: *The class has begun to stir. They are growing restless and losing interest in the lesson.*

Solution: Ask the students to stand and sing the song below to the tune of "Ten Little Indians." Have them whistle (or try to!) after each phrase.

*One little (one whistle), two little (two whistles),
three little whistles (three whistles);
Four little (four whistles), five little (five
whistles), six little whistles (six whistles);
Seven little (seven whistles), eight little
(eight whistles), nine little whistles (nine
whistles),
Ten little whistles now (ten whistles)!*

Ask the children to do it with you. Sing it through twice, then quickly introduce the next portion of the lesson plan.

Desired Result: The class will forget their restlessness, will not need to be scolded, and will be ready to learn again after the break.

Items Needed: None

Idea #4: QUIET SONG

Situation: *The children have been sitting for many minutes and are obviously in need of a change.*

Solution: Quietly sing a song for the children. Then request that they sing it with you. A workable song can be:

> *Let's listen to Jesus,*
> *Let's listen to Jesus,*
> *Let's listen to Jesus,*
> *He speaks to us through His Word.*
> (tune: chorus of "O How I Love Jesus")

Desired Result: Children's attenton is redirected in a pleasant way, and they are not allowed to get bored and misbehave. The relaxing, challenging song will guide them into quietness and attention.

Items Needed: A pre-chosen tune of a familiar song

Idea #5: STANDING LESSON

Situation: *The class has been sitting for more than ten minutes. There may not be a discipline problem yet, but if the children do not get a break, they will find it difficult to sit still.*

Solution: Stop the lesson at a dramatic point. Announce, loudly and clearly, for every student to stand up tall and straight and place their hands on their hips. Then teach a portion of the lesson with the children in that position. After three or four minutes, ask the children to reach for the ceiling, touch their shoulders, toes, and sit down.

Desired Result: The children will be better able to listen, will not misbehave, and will have their hands busy and out of mischief (with no need for scolding!) for at least part of the lesson.

Items Needed: None

Idea #6: OVERHEAD LOOK

Situation: *The teacher wishes to change from one activity to another, or the teacher notices too much noise in the classroom.*

Solution: Before class, set up an overhead projector and write on a transparency: "QUIET" or "LISTEN" or "SIT STILL" in large, attractive letters—you may even want to use a cute illustration. When the moment arrives to quiet the class, turn on the overhead. When all obey, turn it off. You can turn it on again (and again) if necessary. You can also use it to change activities by writing, "STAND UP AND STRETCH." See who notices first and praise the student for being so attentive.

Desired Result: The teacher does not need to yell or raise his/her voice. A silent reminder helps children learn to listen and makes changing activities more of a game to see who notices first.

Items Needed: Overhead Projector
Transparencies
Transparency markers
Illustration for transparency (optional)

Idea #7: WALNUT CHOICE

Situation: *A long teaching session needs to be broken into two segments to avoid restlessness or misbehavior problems.*

Solution: Bring three half-walnut shells (or use three plastic eggs) to class with three prepared suggestions, one under each shell. When appropriate, ask a student to choose a shell, pick it up, and lead the class in what it says. Have another child choose another shell a little later. The third suggestion can wait until another class or another break.

Suggestions for activities might be:
1) Stand up, turn around, reach high, bend low.
2) Sing a motion chorus.
3) Make hands do three activities like: clap, make circles, clap in back of you.
4) Shake hands with five people.
5) Foot activities like: Hop on one foot, hop on the other foot, or jump with both feet.

Desired Result: Students get to move about in an interesting way they enjoy. Walnut (or egg) choices provide opportunities for student leadership, and they help the class be ready to sit still once again for the rest of the class period. Attention increases.

Items Needed: Three half-walnut shells (or three plastic eggs)
Written suggestions to fit under shells (or in eggs)

Idea #8: PICK A CARD

Situation: *The teacher has been teaching a lesson but, after a while, the students begin to squirm and show a lack of interest.*

Solution: Stop at a dramatic place in the lesson. Bring out a pile of prepared cards and lay them face down on the table. A volunteer picks one up and does what it says. That student chooses another student to pick a card and do what it says. Let three or four take part. Leave the rest of the cards for later in the class or another session.

The cards could say:
1) What was the last sentence the teacher said?
2) Shake hands with another student.
3) Touch an open Bible.
4) Say a Bible verse.
5) Exchange chairs with someone.
6) What is the subject of today's lesson?
7) Hum a tune; see who can guess what it is.
8) Hop to the door and back.
9) Stand up, turn around, and sit down.
10) Whistle part of a hymn.
11) Imitate a duck walking into Noah's ark.
12) Act out today's lesson in pantomime.

Desired Result: The students have fun, change their position, and get anxious to continue their lesson.

Items Needed: A stack of index cards with a suggestion written on each

Idea #9: INSTANT MEMORY

Situation: *In the middle of a lesson, when the class gets a little fidgety, you want to calm the children.*

Solution: Announce at the opening of the class session, "Today, I will take a Polaroid picture of each student who is paying attention when the bell rings." Set a kitchen timer for five, eight, or ten minutes (depending on age of students). When the timer sounds, stop teaching, pick up the camera, and take a picture of each child who was truly paying attention. Tell them that if they remain well behaved, they can take their picture home. If one or two couldn't have their picture taken because of a problem, promise another opportunity (a month or two in the future) so they will have another chance.

Desired Result: An awake class, on their best behavior, and listening to the lesson. Remember, good behavior is more than sitting still and listening; it includes hearing and participating.

Items Needed: Polaroid camera, loaded with film
Kitchen timer

Idea #10: COMPLIMENT TREE

Situation: *The class does well in the discipline area. They enjoy their class, pay attention, and seldom misbehave.*

Solution: Place a cardboard tree on the bulletin board and have gummed stars of different colors near by. Every few minutes, when the class is paying attention and participating, let different students decorate the tree with a few stars. Continue the lesson. A little later, repeat the decoration with more stars and different students. The third time, have other students put more stars on the tree if it is appropriate. You can also have each section put different colors on the tree.

Desired Result: The compliment tree rewards good or helpful actions. This reverse discipline compliments the class members for good behavior and is more useful than scolding a misbehaving class.

Items Needed: A cardboard tree
Multi-colored, gummed stars

Idea #11: HIDDEN SUGGESTIONS

Situation: *The teacher realizes the temptation to distract other students.*

Solution: Before class, hide folded papers in inconspicuous places. On the papers, print suggestions such as:

1) Exchange chairs
2) Zip your lip
3) Find a pencil and paper and write: QUIET
4) Hop in place three times
5) Whistle "Jesus Loves Me"
6) Stand up, say, "I will listen" three times, and sit down.
7) Read today's Memory Verse.

Have the students hunt for the papers five or six minutes into the lesson. Then call for suggestion #1 to be read and done. Teach some more, and call for suggestion #2 to be read and done. Continue until all the suggestions are used.

Desired Result: Good behavior and fun in the process.

Items Needed: Several small peices of paper with suggestions printed on them and folded

Idea #12: TINY TREATS

Situation: *The class tries very hard to be good. They succeed.*

Solution: Reward good behavior with a small wrapped candy or toy rather than rewarding misbehavior with a scolding. Have a supply of wrapped candy, toys, even books in the classroom. Half-way through the lesson or at the very end of the class period, give each of the students a treat.

Desired Result: Good behavior is rewarded; the students are happy and the class learns that they can honor the Lord by their obedience (I Samuel 15:22).

Items Needed: A supply of small, wrapped candies and trinkets

Idea #13: MUSICAL CHALK

Situation: *The need for a change of activity is evident after the students have been sitting still for enough minutes for their age limitations.*

Solution: Hand a piece of chalk to a student. Play some music. Pass the chalk around the circle. Whoever has the chalk when the music stops takes the chalk to the chalkboard and writes: "TIME TO PAY ATTENTION AGAIN" or "TIME TO LEARN MORE ABOUT THE BIBLE." Then go back to teaching the lesson.

Desired Result: An attentive, listening, learning, content class.

Items Needed: Music (cassette tape and cassette player)
Chalkboard and chalk, or paper and pen or marker

Idea #14: TIC-TAC-OBEY

Situation: *The class needs a short break to re-focus their attention or a bridge is needed from a noisy activity to a quiet, learning time without discipline problems.*

Solution: Make a large TIC-TAC-TOE grid on the chalkboard or on posterboard.

Divide the class into two sides. Each side, acting as a team, must agree on the placement of their "X" or "O." You can let the game last for one month, if necessary, by giving only two turns per side per week. To take a turn, the side must answer a question relevant to the lesson. If the side doesn't know the answer, they lose a turn and the other side gets a question. Be sure to give the correct answer. Suitable questions might be:
1) Who is the lesson about today?
2) Where is the Bible lesson taking place?
3) What is the Scripture reference for today's lesson?
4) What is one lesson we can learn from this story?

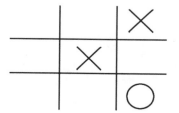

Desired Result: A break, a review, team spirit, fun, and a desire to return week after week. You can give the winning team a small reward.

Items Needed: Posterboard with tic-tac-toe grid, or chalkboard with same

Two markers (different colors)

Idea #15: TIME RELAY

Situation: *The class has been still for a long time. They need to move about before they can't help misbehaving.*

Solution: Have an alarm clock or timer set to go off in six or eight minutes. At the beginning of class, explain the game, dividing the class into two teams. When the timer sounds, the students must stand, form a line, and pass a sponge over their heads to the end of the team and back to the first person. Go back to teaching for another six or eight minutes, then do the relay again, three times during class. A big applause for the winning team is a good reward.

Desired Result: The class has relaxed, moved about, and is willing as well as physically and mentally able to learn during the remainder of the lesson. Teamwork has also been emphasized.

Items Needed: Alarm clock or timer
2 sponges

Idea #16: BEHAVIOR THERMOMETER

Situation: The class tries to behave, but sometimes they forget.

Solution: Make a large thermometer for the classroom. It can be drawn on the chalkboard, made on posterboard, or created on sheets of paper. Label it: *Classroom Behavior*. You could also make a series of smaller thermometers, similarly labeled, and record the date with each one. A month of "good" or better behavior would merit a special class treat.

After half the class period, mark the thermometer honestly: excellent, very good, good, needs improving, poor, awful. Discuss it with the class. At the end of the class, mark it again. Hopefully, it will go up.

Classroom Behavior

Desired Result: The students have a visible reminder to improve their behavior...and they consciously try to listen and learn.

Items Needed: A thermometer (made from posterboard, paper, or drawn on chalkboard)
Chalk or marker

Idea #17: SAND CASTLES

Situation: *Every class needs opportunities to stop, rest, relax, and then continue the lesson.*

Solution: Bring in a basket of sand, a pitcher of water, and a large sheet of plastic. Place the sheet of plastic on the floor. Give each student a scoop of sand, pour a little water on it (or pre-dampen all the sand in advance). Have the students make a church, or Jericho's walls, or Mt. Sinai, the temple, a cross, an empty tomb, or any easily made part of the day's lesson.

Desired Result: Children will enjoy the relaxed, related fun and will be ready and anxious for more teaching.

Items Needed: Basket of sand
Pitcher of water
Large plastic sheet
Spoon or scoop
Picture of object to be made (from lesson or
    elsewhere)

Idea #18: SONG MINUTE

Situation: *Students have been sitting still for a reasonable amount of time and need a break.*

Solution: Find a good point no more than 20 minutes into the class session, and sing a song like this one to the tune of "Blest Be The Tie That Binds" or "O How I Love Jesus."

> *Let's stand and sing a song*
> *About our God of love,*
> *We're learning and doing*
> * and trusting Him,*
> *And we thank our God above.*

Sing it twice (maybe once as a round) and return to the lesson.

Desired Result: An interruption or variation in activity gives the students an opportunity to use muscles, voices, and minds in a relaxing and fun fashion. They soon are ready to study again. Most importantly, the class will avoid misbehavior because they've had a chance to stretch their muscles.

Items Needed: Words to song written on posterboard
Music for class pianist (if one is available)

Idea #19: AIRPLANE RACE

Situation: *The teacher has taught half the lesson and the students have done well. They need to move or they will soon wiggle and lose attention.*

Solution: Half-way through the teaching of a Bible lesson, hand each student a sheet of thin, white paper approximately 4" x 6". Show them how to fold it into a plane and make it able to fly. On the plane they should write the name of a Bible character (other than the names of God, Jesus, or the Holy Spirit). After three minutes, have the students stand and try to "fly" their plane across the room at a paper on the floor designated as the airport with the name of the location of the Bible story on it. Promise them another opportunity to fly their planes before the end of class. Make them leave their planes on the floor until the next opportunity. That way, they won't play with them during the teaching session.

Desired Result: The students will be reminded of the lesson, have relaxation, and enjoy the time. They will be ready and able to continue in the teaching portion of the class period.

Items Needed: 4" x 6" sheets of white paper, one for each student
Large sheet of paper for "airport" with "runways" marked
Pencils or markers for each student

(If you don't know how to fold a paper airplane, be sure to find someone to show you. Your students may already know how!)

Idea #20: SIREN

Situation: *A class has tried its best to listen and learn. They find it hard as time passes.*

Solution: Make, buy, or borrow a recording of a police or fire engine siren. When students get too noisy during a project, a craft, the memorizing or listening time, play the siren. Tell the students they are to quiet down every time they hear the siren. It's the Lesson 911 siren rescuing the Bible lesson from the danger of disruption. Be sure to keep the volume considerate of nearby classes

Desired Result: The class will come to attention and listen without the teacher raising her voice. Tempers are saved, and there is some amusement at the Lesson 911 rescue horn. Be prepared to explain what the real 911 number is for and help students understand how they can get help when/if they're in trouble.

Items Needed: Recording of a siren
Tape player

Idea #21: FLOWER BOUQUET

Situation: *Although the class is generally well behaved, there are occasions when the students need to be reminded to quiet down and listen to God's Word.*

Solution: Bring a large selection of flowers (wild or garden variety). Lay them on wet newspapers. After a portion of the lesson, let the students pause for a project and renew their attention spans. Do this several times, allowing each student to arrange a small bouquet one flower at a time. Let the students take the bouquets home to Mom or give to some of the elderly ladies in an adult class. (This would have to be pre-arranged.)

If real flowers are too expensive, not available, or impractical for other reasons, use artificial ones. You could also make tissue flowers.

Desired Result: The students will feel good about themselves, will be able to do a better job in class participation and listening, and will learn to give as they share the flowers with others after class.

Items Needed: A large selection of flowers (real, artificial, or tissue)
Wet newspaper
A large vase or bucket to hold the live flowers

Idea #22: FINISH THE VERSE

Situation: *Students have been fully involved with the lesson for the limit of their attention span. They need a break.*

Solution: Occasionally, during the lesson, start a Bible verse previously memorized. The class, at the snap of your finger, must repeat the entire verse from memory. Try a second verse with the class standing at attention. Repeat the "Finish the Verse" procedure again in another few minutes. Or, you can start a verse and ask any student to finish it.

Another option is to do a round robin through the class with each student adding the next word in the verse.

Desired Result: The students get a profitable way to change their pace, wiggle, and use their memory verses. A word of praise after they repeat the verse will raise their self-esteem and help them to see value in Scripture memorization.

Items Needed: None

Idea #23: STICKERS

Situation: *The class has restless students but most want to behave and learn the Bible lesson. They find it hard after a number of minutes have elapsed.*

Solution: Provide one sheet of paper (colored paper or construction paper) for each student. They can fold it in half and cut it on the fold. Then they can fold the half pieces in half again, making two books which become sticker albums. Give each student one sticker right away. Explain that they may have more, according to their attention and cooperation in class. You might give out stickers for:

> 1 sticker for participation
> 1 sticker for listening
> 1 sticker for improved behavior
> 2 stickers for learning the Bible verse
> 1 sticker for being quiet

Stickers can be purchased in many stores with many different pictures.

Either have students put the two halves together for an eight-page book or use one four-page book now and save the other half for later.

Desired Result: The desire for stickers, the fun of collecting, the recognition from the teacher makes good behavior worthwhile. Christian stickers with Bible verses and sayings will remain with the students long after class and be noticed at home, as well.

Items Needed: Colored or construction paper, enough for each student
"Safe" scissors for each student
Stickers

Idea #24: CHAIN LINK

Situation: *The class is excited about learning the Bible lesson of the day. They have no intention of performing unacceptable actions, but....*

Solution: Give all the students a piece of light colored paper about 1" x 6". Ask the students to write their good intention about behavior on the paper in large block letters. Have each student make their piece of paper into a link and connect their paper into a long paper chain. Hang it up in the front of the classroom. If someone forgets, ask the student to come forward and read his/her promise to the class.

Desired Result: Most children will decide to behave acceptably and will probably try harder than before. It also reinforces what a promise means. If you wish, you can do a mini-lesson as an aside on what it means to promise God something and what He expects of us when we make Him a promise (Ecclesiastes 5:4-5).

Items Needed: Colored paper, 1" x 6", one for each student
Pen or marker for each student
Glue, stapler, or tape

Idea #25: HANDS ON KNEES

Situation: *Students have been sitting for enough time, but the lesson is not quite finished. They need exercise. If it isn't planned into the program, they will do it in an inappropriate way.*

Solution: When the class is fidgety, don't scold, just say, "Stand up." Wait while they do it, then say, "Hands on knees, hands on hips, hands on toes, hands on head, hands folded, all sit down." You might want to repeat it a couple of times with variations to help them listen more intently.

Desired Result: Fun and exercise allow students to dispose of pent-up energy and make students ready and eager to study and learn again.

Items Needed: None

Idea #26: TIMER

Situation: *There is a hard lesson to teach that takes extra concentration. The teacher fears students will not be able to sit through the whole teaching session.*

Solution: Break up the teaching into three periods. Use a timer! Then the students will realize that they get a break. Encourage them with the promise of something special each time the timer sounds. (It might be a refreshment break; it could be a game.)

Desired Result: Instead of feeling bored and losing interest, the students will see that they can listen, relax...listen, relax...and listen again. They will discover they can learn with short sessions.

Items Needed: A timer
Refreshment, pre-planned game, or other options designed for your class

Idea #27: POEM WRITING

Situation: *Your Bible lesson is well taught, interesting, and worthwhile, but two or three students get tired of listening.*

Solution: Stop while teaching the lesson and have the class write a poem. Begin it with:

```
┌─────────────────────────────────────┐
│  THINGS I WANT TO LEARN TODAY...     │
│                                      │
│  _____    │
│                                      │
│                                      │
│  _____    │
│                                      │
│                                      │
│  _____    │
│                                      │
└─────────────────────────────────────┘
```

Have the students add three more lines. Let every student, especially the disinterested students, help in forming a line. Write it on the chalkboard. When it is done, have all the students repeat it in unison. If the disinterested students don't read with the class, ask them to read it alone. Then go back to teaching without mentioning any wrongdoing. If there are more outbreaks of mischief, have the class read the poem again, or begin a new poem about the lesson content for the students to complete.

Desired Result: The students will think about learning and their reason for being in class.

Items Needed: Chalkboard and chalk

Idea #28: 1000 POINTS

Situation: *You want to stimulate the students' desire to listen from the very beginning of the class session.*

Solution: Have a competition for good actions that please the Lord even more than you, as their teacher. Explain to the class that for every five minutes of acceptable behavior, you will give each student 1000 points. Let them keep their own scores. See who can get the most points and then have something special for those who get more than 6,000 points. If someone misbehaves, deduct 500 points. Be sure the class understands what is acceptable and unacceptable behavior.

Desired Result: Students will enjoy good behavior, keeping their own scores, and the public approval by their teacher.

Items Needed: Paper and pencil for each student

Idea #29: HOPSCOTCH LESSON

Situation: *Students need more than a lecture to learn the day's lesson. They need to involve muscles which are in need of exercise, brains which are tired, and hands which are fidgety.*

Solution: Draw a *hopscotch* diagram on a large piece of paper (at least 2 1/2 feet by 5 feet). Put a score on each square. Let each child have a turn throwing a bean bag onto the paper from the edge of the table. Establish a list of activities for each number. Whatever number the bean bag lands on, the student must perform that activity, such as repeat a memory verse, say the books of the Old Testament, or name the disciples, etc.

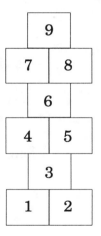

Desired Result: Provides a fun way to review, a break from sitting, and renews minds for listening and learning.

Items Needed: Hopscotch diagram on 2 1/2' x 5' paper
A bean bag
List of numbered activities

Idea #30: FOAM BALL PASS

Situation: *The class has been behaving in a disciplined fashion, but a break must be forthcoming in order to avoid potential discipline problems.*

Solution: Half-way through a teaching session, stand up and throw a small foam ball to one student and say, "Genesis." That student must throw it to another student and yell, "Exodus." The third student must throw the ball to another student and call, "Leviticus," and so on through all the books of the Bible (or just the Old Testament or just the New Testament). If a student makes a mistake, he becomes one-third ($\frac{1}{3}$) of a pumpkin, Christmas tree, baseball, clam or whatever the season may call for. Be sure to explain the game in advance. You can use this game throughout the quarter and students will not have to have it explained twice. It can be spontaneous fun.

Desired Result: An instructional, fun review time along with a change of position, activity, and mindset.

Items Needed: A small foam ball

Idea #31: UP VERSE

Situation: *The class has been listening and behaving for several minutes, but they are getting restless and seem unable to grasp more information.*

Solution: This game works if the students are sitting around a table. Have a small piece of cardboard, about ½" x 1" (folded in half), and write on it a Bible verse to be remembered. Each participant puts his/her hands under the table. The students pass around the card with the Bible verse. When you call, "UP VERSE," the students all put their arms up, elbows on the table and their hands closed in a fist, concealing what might be in there. The teacher guesses who has the card. If you guess correctly, the student reads the verse and becomes "it." The students again put their hands under the table, pass the card until "it" says, "UP VERSE." "It" guesses and if correct, the person with the card reads it and becomes "it." Play three or four times.

Desired Result: Better behavior without scolding and a fun way to learn.

Items Needed: A small piece of cardboard, 1/2 " x 1" with a Bible verse written on it.

Idea #32: PRAISE IN CHURCH

Situation: *The class is well behaved and deserves praise. An occasional outbreak of silliness or inattention is not grounds for avoiding this praise in church.*

Solution: During the morning church service, if time is allotted for public praise, give praise to God for the great Sunday School class you teach. If it is not done at the morning service, there will probably be an opportunity at an evening service, a prayer meeting, or even the opening session of Sunday School. Let everyone know how proud you are of the class and how they are pleasing God in their learning process.

Desired Result: The class will be happy to hear what the teacher thinks of them and will try to live up to their good reputation. They will also realize afresh that they are responsible to God and that He knows and appreciates their efforts in class.

Items Needed: None

Idea #33: BEADS

Situation: *The class is well behaved, happy, and learning. They don't intend to do things that would displease the teacher or the Lord.*

Solution: Let the class have fun as they add up their good actions. Hang a long string at the front of the classroom. Tie a double knot at the end of it. Each time the students accomplish something, act very good, answer a question, or fill in a page, put a bead on the string. Let different students add the beads. If the string with beads gets long enough to put around your neck like a necklace, or your waist like a belt, reward the students with a game, a sticker, or a small snack. Then be sure to wear it.

Desired Result: The students will have fun while they learn and will want to do more to increase the length of the bead string. They will learn their verses, enter into discussions, listen to the story, study their workbooks, look up Bible verses, just for an opportunity to add a bead.

Items Needed: A long string, 30" or more
Beads, enough to fill the length of string
A "reward"

Idea #34: STUDENT OF THE DAY

Situation: *The class is normal: well behaved most of the time, poorly behaved only some of the time.*

Solution: Use this method for one month. At the end of the first class in the month, select a *Student of the Day*. It can be someone well behaved (not angelic). Let it be someone who actively participated in the class, listened carefully to the teacher, asked good questions, and was kind to other students. That person can wear a special pin (or hat for younger students). At the next class, the *Student of the Day* is in charge of discipline and speaks to those who do not act in a proper manner. At the end of the class, that *Student of the Day* and the teacher confer to decide who will be the next *Student of the Day*. At the end of the third session, both previous *Students of the Day* confer with the teacher for the next *Student of the Day*. This should be a once a year event and something special. Don't do it all the time. It would soon lose its effect.

Desired Result: Students will try to behave while they also try to take an active part in the class. Good discipline does not consist of students sitting and staring at the teacher...it consists of active, listening, participating students.

Items Needed: Special pin or hat

Idea #35: MOVE ONE

Situation: *The class is noisy, disinterested, and paying little or no attention to the teacher.*

Solution: The teacher must get the class's attention. This can be done with a handclap, a note on the piano, a raised hand, or a soft, firm, "Quiet, please." Then say; "Everyone please stand. Move one space to the chair to your right. Okay. Sit down and listen to the next exciting part of our lesson." Be prepared with some creative change in the lesson, to paper work, a song, a role play, a visual, an object lesson, or a Bible game. (For ideas on Bible games, see my book, *Learning Games and Activities*.)

Desired Result: A new chair and a new opportunity to behave can help a child listen better and enjoy the class. A change means a new start, and the students who were obnoxious may cease for long enough to gain interest in the rest of the class and the lesson.

Items Needed: A pre-planned creative activity—paper work, a song, role play, visual, object lesson, or Bible game.

Idea #36: BLOW YOUR HORN

Situation: *The children are bored and restless, learning has come to a standstill.*

Solution: Give small play horns to all the students in the first row, or on the left side of the table, or all the boys, or all the girls. When the noise level gets *loud*, or when there isn't enough to do, give a pre-arranged signal to the horn blowers and let them BLOW THEIR OWN HORNS. Announce that this is the signal to quiet down and listen for a special activity to come up immediately. (For ideas on object lessons, see *Bible Object Lessons* by Mary Rose Pearson or my book mentioned in Idea #35.)

Desired Result: The class will have fun quieting down; there will be no need for discipline, and the new activity will begin with eagerness.

Items Needed: Five or six toy musical horns

Idea #37: SNAP, WIGGLE, CLAP

Situation: *The students can't help it; some are wiggling, giggling, bothering other students, whispering, and generally uninterested in the lesson.*

Solution: Without anger and without scolding anyone, pause! Look at each student with a smile and say, "Hold it a minute. Before the rest of the story, let's play a game. It's called, *snap, wiggle, clap.*" Explain that every time you, the teacher, say the word, HELP, the students must snap their fingers. Every time you say the word LISTEN, the students must wiggle. Every time you say the word, SILLY, the students are to clap their hands. Have them practice.

Then tell a funny story, something like this:

One day, there was a crowd of silly children who needed help, but they wouldn't listen. Did you hear me? They wouldn't listen. They needed help to listen. They were the silly children of (your town). They were silly at breakfast; they were silly at noon time; they were silly and needed help but they would not listen. They really needed help to listen! Yes, they needed help to listen!

Vary the loudness of your voice each time you say, "They needed help to listen."

Desired Result: The children get rid of their silliness, their wiggles, and have something to listen for, helping them to be ready once again to listen to the lesson.

Items Needed: None

Idea #38: GIGGLE CLOTH

Situation: *Some of the students are giggling; they can't seem to stop. The harder they try, the more uncontrollable the giggling becomes.*

Solution: Have a brightly colored cloth handy. When there is too much giggling, hold the cloth high and say, "Giggle. Every one of you. Right now." Be sure to join them with your heartiest giggle.

Then, explain that they can giggle while the cloth is in the air, but when the cloth touches the floor, they must be silent. Toss the cloth into the air, giggle with the students for the time it takes the cloth to reach the floor, then stop immediately. Do it several times. If the students can't stop when the cloth reaches the floor, write their name on the chalkboard under the designation of "1/3 of a silly bird."

Desired Result: The children will get over their silliness and be ready to settle down again and listen to the rest of the lesson. Use this method only occasionally, and it will serve its intended purpose.

Items Needed: A brightly colored cloth
Chalkboard and chalk, or paper and pen or marker

Idea #39: TREASURE BOX

Situation: *Children are tired of sitting, seem tired of listening to the teacher, and are misbehaving.*

Solution: Whisper the word, "Quiet" and when the kids are silent, tell about your treasure box. You'll need to prepare it ahead with enough small gifts for each of the children. They can be wrapped so no one can tell what they are. They should be small, inexpensive items such as a wrapped candy, a pencil, a pad of paper, a motto button, a bookmark, a magnet.

Announce that everyone who can sit still during the rest of the lesson and not talk unless asked to participate can have a piece of treasure. Then continue the lesson.

If the children are quiet, follow through and let them make their choices from the treasure box. If some make noises or move around when they aren't supposed to, be firm: no gift from the treasure box.

Desired Result: The children will make a real effort to pay attention to the rest of the lesson. Don't make the time of "being good" longer than a few minutes or beyond the reach of the class. Be sensitive to age level attention spans.

Items Needed: A box decorated like a "treasure box"
Several small, wrapped gifts, one for each student and a few extras for any visitors

Idea #40: I WILL, I WILL NOT

Situation: *The students are taking advantage of the teacher, fooling around and not listening. There is disruption from some members of the class.*

Solution: Either before the lesson or when the problem occurs, write several sentences like these on the chalkboard:

1) I will listen when the teacher is talking.
2) I will not talk when the teacher is talking.
3) I will pay attention to my teacher.
4) I will not be disrespectful to my teacher.
5) I will help others listen to our lesson.

Then, start with the student to your right. He/she must say an "I will" sentence from the chalkboard. The next student to the right must say an "I will not" sentence. Continue around the entire class. Each one must say one of the sentences, every other one saying, "I will," the next saying an "I will not" sentence. If the students begin fooling around again during the lesson, stop teaching and repeat this same class activity.

Desired Result: An instant change of attitude without singling out individuals. It lets the entire class know that such behavior is not acceptable. Also, the Bible lesson can continue in a learning atmosphere.

Items Needed: Chalkboard and chalk, or paper and pen or marker

Idea #41: LIGHT FLICK

Situation: *The class has become noisy, not naughty, but disruptive. The noise is beyond what is acceptable.*

Solution: This could be one of your stated class procedures for reminding students who get too noisy that it's time to settle down. Or, before class, announce that when it becomes too noisy, you will not speak, but merely flick the lights off and on several times. When the occasion arises, do what you promised and do not mention the problem. It should cause quieter behavior. If not, you needn't tell the students to be quiet, just say, "Who remembers what the *Light Flick* is for?" Have someone answer and usually the students will automatically resume a quiet atmosphere. Any student who doesn't quiet down can merely be touched on the shoulder and usually he/she will react positively.

Desired Result: A non-threatening discipline has been enforced, and the offenders have been able to correct their behavior without a public scolding. All try to be quieter for the benefit of the entire class and nearby classes.

Items Needed: A light with a switch

Idea #42: COVER YOUR MOUTH

Situation: *The class has begun talking and giggling and needs to be quiet.*

Solution: At a noisy moment in class, stop talking and write on the chalkboard: When I cover my mouth with the palm of my hand, every student is to copy me.

Pause and do so. Without scolding, stand still until all the students copy you. Then, remove your hand while you make announcements or continue teaching. Students will uncover their mouths, too. Be sure to allow the students further opportunity to talk quietly when it will not disturb the lesson, but keep those moments completely quiet.

Desired Result: Quiet, but you do not have to yell or create hurt feelings. The class will automatically quiet down and learn that there are times to be quiet and times to talk.

Items Needed: Chalkboard and chalk, or paper and pen or marker

Idea #43: RECORDER RESULTS

Situation: *The children need reminders from time to time to pay attention to the teacher. There are times for sharing with each other, and there are times to listen.*

Solution: During a class when there is extra time, or in a pre-session, record some interesting suggestions for classroom behavior. With some quiet background music, let a student record words like: "Now it is time to be very quiet and listen to the teacher." Or, "Now it is time to talk quietly while we do our work." Then, play some action music or marching music and let a student record words like: "It is all right to move around the room if we want to," Or, "It is time to sit at the table and do our crafts." You can play the recorder, with the child's instructions, whenever it is time to change an activity.

Desired Result: A happy transition from one activity to another without yelling or loud talk. Children hear themselves or their friends, and it is a fun reminder of what happens next.

Items Needed: Cassette recorder/player with microphone
Cassette with a variety of pre-taped music (relaxing, marching, etc.)

Idea #44: GOOD CAP

Situation: *Students get carried away; they get silly, boisterous, out of hand, and don't seem to be able to get back under control.*

Solution: As the class gets noisy, the teacher can put on a cap that says "GOOD" on it. Then notice a well-behaved student and let him/her wear the hat. After several minutes, discover another "GOOD" student. Have the first student place the cap on him/her. Keep the hat moving. Try to find a student who struggles with sitting still and listening. If such a student tries hard, let him/her wear the cap and tell that one how pleased you are with his/her good behavior.

Desired Result: There should be a real effort to behave and pay attention in order to receive special recognition for it—rather than a reprimand for the wrong actions in class.

Items Needed: A cap with "GOOD" printed or taped on the front

Idea #45: MIRROR PRINT

Situation: *There are several students who refuse to listen, participate, or be a part of the class.*

Solution: In the teaching area, have a small mirror, perhaps four by six inches, handy. When someone does an unacceptable action, silently take the mirror to the person and hold it in front of the student. Don't say a word. Repeat the procedure if another child misbehaves. Take it back to the same student if necessary. Soon everyone will realize what the mirror is for.

Desired Result: The misbehaving students will begin to act in an appropriate manner. You will help them to see their actions as a reflection of themselves and change a student's behavior.

Items Needed: A small hand mirror

Idea #46: PLEASE TOWER

Situation: *The class doesn't obey the "Quiet" command or the "Listen" suggestion. They continue doing their own thing while the teacher is teaching.*

Solution: Keep a half dozen blocks from the nursery department in your classroom with simple commands written on paper taped to them. One block may say, "QUIET," another "LISTEN," another "PAY ATTENTION," another "WHY," another "SHHHH," and another "HUSH." As the lesson starts, put one block in front of the class. If they forget, add a block, then another. When it is time for another activity, let a quiet student take out the bottom block! Everyone will enjoy seeing them fall.

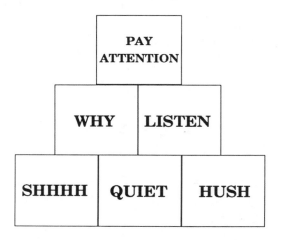

Desired Result: The students will have fun acting in a correct manner and see that minding, listening, and learning are more fun than acting up.

Items Needed: Six children's blocks with behavioral commands taped to them

Idea #47: BEST CHAIR

Situation: *Some students seek attention by fooling around during serious times in class. Some enjoy doing the opposite of what the teacher desires.*

Solution: Provide—not a naughty chair—but a special GOOD CHAIR. You could have a bean bag chair or a "papa san" chair in one corner of the classroom and decorate it like a throne. Select a well-behaved student to bring it into the class circle and to sit in it. Ten minutes later, select another good student, and still another for the next ten minutes (if the lesson lasts that long.) If a student who is usually unable to act appropriately improves dramatically, give him/her the chair and a big round of applause, or for those who are shyer, a big smile.

Desired Result: The students will feel good about themselves. They will strive for better behavior when they are recognized for their accomplishments.

Items Needed: A "special" or unique chair

Idea #48: SCREW UP

Situation: *The class begins to whisper, wiggle, giggle, and not pay attention when it is time for serious Bible study.*

Solution: If students have a habit of misbehaving, bring a screwdriver, a large screw, and a small block of wood to class.

Say to the students, "When you are acting in the right way, we'll turn this screw. Let's see if we can get it all the way into the block of wood before the end of the class." You can give it a twist and say, "Now try to listen to every word of the lesson." In about five minutes compliment the class and turn the screw. Repeat the action about every five minutes, letting different children turn the screw. By the end of class, the screw should be all the way into the wood, and an enthusiastic teacher can start a round of applause.

Desired Result: A class becomes happier as it learns to behave. They work together to learn the lesson.

Items Needed: Screwdriver
Screw
Block of wood

Idea #49: WRITE THE RULE

Situation: *The class finds itself restless, with their minds wandering from the lesson subject.*

Solution: Point out the previously established list of rules or expectations for the class behavior. (See Idea #3.) The rules need to be posted on the bulletin board so you can point to them when necessary.

Remember to keep them simple, clear, and as few as possible for young minds. At the moment of disinterest, gather the students' interest by calling out in a loud voice, "Attention!" Hand out plain paper and pencils. Point out the rule being broken: *We will listen to our teacher when the lesson is being taught.* Rewrite that one rule on the chalkboard in large letters. Have students print the rule on their papers. Ask the worst offender (without classifying the student as such) to read the paper to the class when the work is completed. Ask another student to explain it. Then, without criticism or comment, plunge back into the lesson in an excited and interesting manner.

Desired Result: The students should realize their problem, their lack of attention, and their misbehavior. They should quickly get back into the lesson and learn what you are teaching them. There becomes no need for real scolding!

Items Needed: List of rules from Idea #1
Paper and pencils, enough for each student
Chalkboard and chalk, paper and pen or marker

Idea #50: GLASSES

Situation: *The students talk about non-essentials and miss the meaning of the lesson.*

Solution: Make a special pair of sunglasses. Put a sign on one-half of the sunglasses. It could say, "QUIET" or "LISTEN." When the class gets off track or shows a lack of attention, you need not scold or raise your voice. Just put on the glasses until everyone gets the message—then take them off and continue teaching. Repeat if necessary.

Or, you could write the lesson topic on white adhesive tape and place it across the bottom of the glasses. Another idea is to use half-glasses and wear them for the next few moments with tape across them giving the lesson truth.

Desired Result: A quick and happy return to attention and the subject.

Items Needed: Sunglasses or half-glasses with a message taped on them

Idea #51: REPORT CARD

Situation: Some students are up and down. They want to do what is right, but they are easily led astray by other students.

Solution: During a one month period, try a report card. It should not necessarily be a continuing project because students could become discouraged and not come again. But for four weeks, there might be an upswing in learning and in a disciplined direction. The report card could include:

Score 1-5 (1 being the best)

Area	Date	Score	Date	Score	Date	Score	Date	Score
Bible Knowledge	9/4	1	9/11	2	9/18	1	9/25	1
Bible Memory	9/4	2	9/11	3	9/18	2	9/25	2
Music	9/4	2	9/11	3	9/18	1	9/25	2
Behavior	9/4	4	9/11	3	9/18	1	9/25	2
Class Participation	9/4	1	9/11	2	9/18	4	9/25	1
Friendly	9/4	1	9/11	2	9/18	1	9/25	1
On Time	9/4	2	9/11	1	9/18	2	9/25	2

Name

In the process, find something good to report about each student—even if it is just being on time regularly, or friendly, or active!

Desired Result: Most students will work for a good report card and an opportunity for the teacher to praise the improving class member. The teacher will also get to share the student's progress with parents.

Items Needed: Design a report card, one for each student

Idea #52: SMILES

Situation: *Unhappy students are usually the ones who misbehave. Sometimes, they don't know how to stop and are afraid of changing their image.*

Solution: Smile! Smile at individual students; smile at good students, smile at misbehaving students, and every time someone seems to be distracted, say their name, make eye contact, and smile.

Desired Result: Students will react to the smiles and the joy of the teacher. That attitude may be the means of making happier students as well as better Christians.

Items Needed: One genuine smile

Idea #53: FLASHCARDS

Situation: *A lack of attention has developed in the classroom.*

Solution: Make three flashcards (16" x 20" approximately) with these captions:

QUIET	LISTEN	LEARN

Prop one of the cards on the table via an easel or other backrest or place silently on a bulletin board when necessary. Snap your fingers to attract attention to the flashcard.

Desired Result: The class comes back into focus with no harsh words, no raised voice, no anger. The class happily pays attention to the rest of the lesson with a gentle reminder.

Items Needed: Three 16" x 20" flashcards
Easel (or other backrest)

Idea #54: COIN FLIP

Situation: *One student is acting silly.*

Solution: Call an offending student (without identifying him/her as bad) to the front of the class. Ask the student to flip a coin for you. If it lands on HEADS, everyone in the class must change chairs. If it lands on TAILS, the entire class must stand on one foot while the student who flipped the coin counts to ten. Then return immediately to the lesson.

Desired Result: The class will get a break and the misbehaving student will change his/her behavior without even realizing it. If he/she continues to act silly while flipping the coin, ask the student to sit on the front row or closest to you and find the key theme in the lesson. The student should calm down, listen, and learn.

Items Needed: A coin

Idea #55: LITTLE COOKIES

Situation: *Most students are well behaved; some are not. Too often, the students who do not act properly get the attention.*

Solution: Make or buy miniature cookies. Every ten minutes (or eight or six, depending on the age and attention spans of the students) give out a cookie to all the well-behaved students. Encourage those who don't qualify the first time to improve so they can get a cookie at the next break. If some students are borderline the first time, let the class decide if they qualify. But be stricter at the second break. Be sure to give specific directions on how you expect their behavior to change in order to get a cookie.

Desired Result: Students are rewarded for good actions and those with less than desirable behavior will try to improve their actions.

Items Needed: A bag of miniature cookies

Idea #56: CRY TEARS

Situation: *The students are not paying attention. Something must be done quickly in order to rescue the teaching part of the session.*

Solution: The teacher takes on the role of an actor. Put on a pantomine skit, pretending to cry and moan and to be completely shattered by the noise and actions of the class. Enlist a couple of well-behaved students to join you. The class should not only get the point, but also enjoy the process of seeing themselves as they have been behaving. Appeal to the children's innate sense of honesty.

Desired Result: A class realizes their unacceptable behavior, changes their ways, and begins to listen to the lesson again. Those who pay attention learn the most.

"Give attention to a wise man, and he will be yet wiser: teach a just man, and he will increase in learning" (Proverbs 9:9).

Items Needed: None

Option: Write the Scripture above on the chalkboard or 3 x 5 cards and give one to each student.

Idea #57: UNREADY TEDDY

Situation: *Some of the students prefer to mess around rather than pay attention or cooperate with the activities.* There may be several reasons for the behavior. Be sure to check out: Room temperature—is it too hot, too cold? Is the teaching session too long for the age group? Is the lesson told in too advanced a manner? Are the chairs too close together, the wrong size, or some other reason? Discipline may still be needed, even after corrective steps are taken for any physical problems.

Solution: Bring a teddy bear to class. Call him, "UNREADY TEDDY." Every time the class acts in a way that makes for poor teaching and learning, bring out *Unready Teddy* and have him say, "What's going on here?" or "I'm ready to learn, aren't you?" or "Let's listen or we'll miss the lesson." Make it amusing and let the children enjoy *Unready Teddy* before plunging back into the lesson. *Unready Teddy* can be used as many times as necessary...after a few times, you may also just be able to set him on a table or ask the worst offender to hold him for you. If students misbehave just to see *Unready Teddy*, change his name to "Ready Teddy," and his comments, too.

Desired Result: You don't have to scold the class. The teddy bear does it for you.

Items Needed: A teddy bear

Idea #58: SILENT CHECKER

Situation: *Students are finding it hard to pay attention while the lesson is being taught.*

Solution: Bring a checkerboard to class and put it on a table. Divide the students into two teams (one side of the room becomes team "A", the other side becomes team "B"). Before you begin teaching, explain that you will be calling on each team during the lesson to answer questions on something just taught. During the lesson, point to any student on team "A" and ask that student a question relevant to the lesson. If he answers the question correctly, he takes a turn on the checkerboard. If he cannot answer it, team "A" gets no turn. Give the correct answer and begin to teach again. In a few minutes, point to a student on team "B" and ask that student a question about the lesson. If the student can answer the question, he takes a turn on the checkerboard or forfeits a turn. Try to balance questions between those who are obviously paying attention and those who aren't. You can also just go straight down the row of each team. As few as 2 students can play this game simply alternating questions. Students will quickly realize that they cannot play unless they are paying attention.

Desired Result: A listening class, enjoying the process of gathering Biblical knowledge, and discovering teamwork in a skill game in the process. If there isn't a checkers winner that week, hold the game over until the following week.

Items Needed: Checkerboard
Checkers
Questions from the lesson

Idea #59: STRAWS

Situation: *The class is silly, disinterested, and unwilling to settle down.*

Solution: Bring in a box of paper straws. Announce at the beginning of the lesson that each time someone misbehaves in some way, you will give him/her a straw. Anyone with two or more straws at the end of the lesson part of the class will not get to share in the refreshment break (or other special treat of the class). Hand out straws without any additional comment.

Desired Result: The class will improve its actions as it sees some get straws. They will also learn self-control and that they can control their behavior. Do not embarrass any student but be firm. Help students learn that there are consequences for negative behavior.

Items Needed: Box of paper straws
Treats for after the lesson

Idea #60: BEHAVIOR SCRABBLE ®

Situation: *Children seem to feel that time at church is time to fool around and take advantage of an inexperienced teacher.*

Solution: Before class begins, place Scrabble® letters on the center of the table, right side up. Ask the children to pick a word that will help them behave during class. When each has his/her word spelled out, count up the score on the letters. Biggest score gets a good round of applause.

Desired Result: The students will know lots of words that will remind them how to act and will have fun reminding themselves.

Items Needed: Scrabble® letters

Idea #61: JUMBLES

Situation: *Some students aren't listening, and they are trying to distract others.*

Solution: Stop teaching. Write scrambled letters on the chalkboard. Praise the one who figures out the word. Repeat it twice and continue teaching. Suggested jumbled words are:

NLSIET (listen)	**TUQEI (quiet)**
YPA TTTANEION (pay attention)	**IST ISTLL (sit still)**

You can add others.

Desired Result: Children get the message in a unique, interesting, and fun way without harsh words.

Items Needed: Chalkboard and chalk, or paper and pen or marker

Idea #62: PASTOR TALK

Situation: *The class is noisy and disobedient to a new teacher.*

Solution: Ask the pastor to visit the class for just a few minutes and give the students a pep-talk (much like a coach would before a game). Let him praise the children, "You are a great group of kids, ordinarily." Then have him make a request that appeals to their budding maturity and sense of responsibility. "Please act properly with your new teacher. He (or she) is new at teaching your class and needs double your attention. Thanks." He can add a quick spiritual reminder, too, by saying something like, "Proper actions please the Lord." He could then lead the children in prayer in dedication of the class members, the teacher, and their time together to the Lord.

Desired Result: The class will see that the pastor cares about them, too. Most of the class members will try to be better behaved to please their pastor, their teacher, and, especially, the Lord.

Items Needed: A willing pastor!

Idea #63: CIRCLE CARD

Situation: *Students like to learn interesting lessons, but sometimes act silly or boldly when it is very inappropriate.*

Solution: Make up cards, one for each student, with a place for a name and numbers from 1–20:

Name_____

1 – 2 – 3 – 4 – 5 – 6 – 7 – 8 – 9 – 10 – 11 – 12 – 13 – 14 – 15 – 16 – 17 – 18 – 19 – 20

Teacher_____
Date_____

Explain at the beginning of the lesson that each student will have a number from 1–20 (20 being the highest) on their card circled with a grade for their behavior. Be sure to remind the class what "good" behavior means to you. At the end of the session, mark the grades. Sign them, and then congratulate the students as they head for home. For those who had low marks, give them a big hug, a pat on the back, or words of encouragement with the assurance that you know they'll do better next time. Do this for at least four weeks.

Desired Result: The desire for a high grade will push students toward good behavior. It will avoid a lot of reprimand and keep a happy class.

Items Needed: Four pre-made cards (as shown above) for each student

Idea #64: NUMBERED CHAIRS

Situation: *Close friends sit next to each other and whisper during the lesson.*

Solution: Before class, place a number under each chair. Write the same numbers on small pieces of paper to correspond with the chair numbers. Place all of the folded slips with numbers on them in a box, basket, or pile. At the beginning of class, let students pick a number from the pile, then have them find the corresponding chair. They must sit there during the class.

Desired Result: With a new seating arrangement, away from friends, all will behave better and learn more. It's also a good opportunity for new friendships and working groups during team activities.

Items Needed: Numbers written on paper and pre-placed under chairs with tape

Corresponding numbers on separate pieces of paper

A box or basket

Idea #65: FUNNY SMILE

Situation: *The students begin to giggle. They aren't being bad; they are just plain silly and can't seem to stop. They won't listen to directions.*

Solution: Draw a large mouth with many teeth on the chalkboard. Each time someone fails to follow directions or you see someone giggle or act silly, pause and blacken one tooth with a piece of chalk. Smile or laugh, don't scold, but tell the students they are taking the smile away by their actions. Then get serious and continue teaching the lesson. There will be enough teeth on the mouth to do this many times, but, hopefully, after three or four times, the class will get the message.

Desired Result: The students will realize that the teacher is human, can laugh as well as they can, and also that there is a time when giggling and laughing needs to be put aside—especially during the teaching of God's Word.

Items Needed: Chalkboard and chalk

Idea #66: QUIET SILENCE

Situation: *The class has become noisy, disruptive, and restless.*

Solution: Stop teaching. Look into the eyes of each student. Tell the class that you are pausing for a game called "Quiet Silence." Tell them:

Quiet Silence has just started;
No student's lips can be parted.
If I hear you talk today,
A forfeit you must do my way.

Explain that if you catch anyone making a noise, you'll snap your fingers, and the person who was talking will have to pay a forfeit. Have in mind several forfeits like:

- whistle a song
- imitate a cat
- walk like a duck
- say a poem
- skip around the room
- say the memory verse
- skip around the room
- hold hands high and count to ten

Print the forfeits on small pieces of paper, fold them in half, and place them on the table. Repeat the rhyme once, then announce, "The game has begun." When a student is caught talking, making noise, etc., that child takes a forfeit and does what is written on it.

Desired Result: The break in routine will give the students a legitimate opportunity to laugh, a break from listening to the lesson, fun, and physical refreshment.

Items Needed: Several small pieces of paper with pre-written forfeits

Idea #67: HIDDEN BUTTON

Situation: *The students are in a silly mood right from the beginning of class. Whatever the teacher says or does strikes the students as funny.*

Solution: Prepare a button with a short, helpful Bible verse printed on a piece of paper and taped to it. Before class or during an activity, hide the button. When the class is acting too silly to learn, announce, "Time for the button game." At the count of three, have the students look for the button. The one who finds it must repeat the Bible verse printed on it. He or she then hides it while all eyes are closed. The students look for it again, and the one who finds it explains what the Bible verse on it means, and returns the button to the teacher for another day.

Desired Result: A break, a chance to get out of a silly rut, and an opportunity to refocus their minds on what God's Word means to them.

Items Needed: A large button (it can be made from paper or cardboard) with a Bible verse printed on it

Idea #68: PRAISE ROUND

Situation: *The students try to be good, but one giggles, another joins in, and soon the class is doing the opposite of what it wants to do.*

Solution: Do not scold the class. Tell them that laughter and happiness are of the Lord. Then go around the class and ask each one to give a praise to the Lord. The teacher begins with something like: "I praise the Lord for bringing each one of you to class today." Then let the others add their praises. Be prepared to help students with ideas for praise.

Desired Result: Students realize God's goodness, joy, and love for them. Also, they receive a break from the regular routine, have an opportunity to get over the giggles, and get ready for serious teaching.

Items Needed: None

Idea #69: BACKWARD COMMANDS

Situation: *Occasionally during the lesson, someone makes a wisecrack or pesters another student.*

Solution: Be prepared. Decide on three desired behaviors and learn to say them backward. Choose any commands you desire, but three easier ones might be:

        teiuq (quiet)
        netsil (listen)
        tis llits (sit still)

Be able to say the words immediately when a situation arises. Do not struggle over them. Let the students guess what you mean. When they do, smile and go on with the lesson or activity. If you wish, you could practice the name of each student in your class backward, also, in front of the other jumbled word.

Desired Result: Keep a smile on your face, and the students will respond. There will be happy cooperation.

Items Needed: None

Idea #70: PRAYER PAUSE

Situation: *The class needs help. They seem to be rude, undisciplined, unhappy, and grouchy.*

Solution: When you notice this attitude, pause before continuing the teaching session. Tell the students, "We are going to spend some time in prayer. It will be silent prayer first, then I will pray. Anyone else can pray after me." Then bow your head in prayer. One by one, the students should stop their actions and be quiet. Finally, pray outloud and ask God to help you and the class get the most from the Bible lesson and that the students will pay attention to God's Word and learn what God has for them. Announce that anyone else can pray, if they desire. Continue in prayer for several seconds but be prepared to end the prayer time reverently whether or not anyone else prays. Many times students will not pray aloud. Get back into the lesson as soon as appropriate.

Desired Result: The students will realize that God is listening, and He doesn't like their actions. Some will confess their bad behavior; all will be aware of why it is wrong to disrupt the class.

Items Needed: None

Idea #71: BOOKMARK

Situation: *The class begins to fuss when the teaching session is hard or long.*

Solution: Make a bookmark for each child. On it have them print:

```
I Praise God.
I listen.
I behave.
I learn in...
Sunday School
Youth Group
Bible Club
```

At appropriate moments during the class, compliment your class members on what they are doing. Remind them of past successes. If the class gets out of hand during the lesson, ask someone to read the bookmark. Then alternate at a well-behaved moment, and ask another student to read theirs.

Desired Result: The students will want to behave and their bookmarks will help remind them why behaving is important. The process gives them praise that they will want to live up to.

Items Needed: A pre-made bookmark for each child
Markers or crayons

Idea #72: SHOES OFF

Situation: *The class looks like it is paying attention, but most of the students are daydreaming.*

Solution: Teach via questions. Everytime a student misses the question, he or she must take off a shoe. Anyone who has both shoes on at the end of the class is a winner and receives a small prize. Hug those with one shoe on and those with both shoes off and ask them to listen more carefully at the next class.

Desired Result: The students will have fun, will pay attention, and will do more than sit still. They will realize that they need to pay attention as well as be quiet. Be careful not to embarrass any child who may have holes in their socks.

Items Needed: A small "prize" for those who still have both shoes on
A hug

Idea #73: ADDITION

Situation: *A class is restless and needs a break in the middle of the teaching session.*

Solution: Choose some phrases that correlate with the lesson such as: Moses led God's people, or Jesus used God's Word to escape temptation, or the boy shared his lunch. Give the phrase and a code to the class:

A=1	F=6	K=11	P=16	U=21
B=2	G=7	L=12	Q=17	V=22
C=3	H=8	M=11	R=18	W=23
D=4	I=9	N=14	S=19	X=24
E=5	J=10	O=15	T=20	Y=25
				Z=26

Let the students figure out how many points they have with their phrase. "The boy shared his lunch" would be:

20 + 8 + 5 = 33	THE
2 + 15 + 25 = 42	BOY
19 + 8 + 1 + 18 + 5 + 4 = 55	SHARED
8 + 9 + 19 = 36	HIS
12+ 21 + 14 + 3 + 8 = 58	LUNCH

Answer: 33 + 42 + 55 + 36 + 58 = 224.

Desired Result: Fun with figures, parts of the lesson to remember, a break in the teaching, and a happy class result from this kind of addition.

Items Needed: Paper and pen
1 set of codes on small sheets of paper for each student
Small calculator

Idea #74: CHORDS AND DISCHORDS

Situation: *A class gets distracted by several students, and there is discord during the teaching session.*

Solution: Play some awful dischords on the piano. Play them loud and continuously until there is quiet. Then explain that the students sound like those dischords. Then play a beautiful chord. Explain, "That is how we should sound during class." Play the dischords once more and ask, "Do you want to be like that?" Then play a musical chord and ask, "Or like this?"

Desired Result: The students will realize their behavior is unpleasant and try to be more like the beautiful chords. There doesn't need to be any scolding, just chords and dischords.

Items Needed: A piano (any instrument will work if there is no piano in the room)

Idea #75: CATCH A FISH

Situation: *There are students who would rather be anywhere else than in class. Because the class is not their first choice, they act in a disagreeable manner.*

Solution: Get a fish bowl (or any large glass bowl) and set it on a table in front of the class. Have small, paper fish in it with paper clips on each fish. Print phrases on each one like:

"Let's be quiet."

"Let's listen to the teacher."

"This Bible story is very important."

"Jesus is listening."

"God wants us to learn about Him during the Bible story."

Make a fishing rod out of a dowel stick about two feet long. Add a string and put a magnet on the end of the string instead of a hook. Whenever someone interrupts the class, ask a student nearest the window, or a student with sneakers on, or whatever, to come and fish. Try to choose a student who is behaving sometimes, but other times choose one who is not acting properly. When they catch a fish, they must read what is on the fish. Go fishing five or six times during class or whenever attention lags.

Desired Result: The students will have fun; they will discipline themselves, and attention and learning will be improved.

Items Needed: A fish bowl (or large glass bowl)

Small, paper fish with phrases printed on them

Paper clips

"Fishing rod" (dowel stick with string and magnet attached)

Idea #76: EVERYONE STARE

Situation: *One or two students refuse to quit misbehaving. They are making the lesson time difficult for both the teacher and the students and have done this frequently.*

Solution: Announce that from the time you snap your fingers, an EVERYONE STARES session starts. That means that you and the students will all stare at any student who is doing something to disrupt the class. If a student makes repeated noises or actions that make teaching impossible, you should stop teaching and stare at the student(s) responsible for the disruption. All the other children are to stop what they are doing and stare at the student(s), too. Count to ten. Then immediately continue the lesson without reprimanding the student(s). If another situation happens, repeat the same process. Soon, no student will want to be stared at; they will all try to pay attention. Make sure the staring lasts no more than to the count of ten and that no student is scolded in any other way. A hug at the end of the lesson for those who misbehaved will reassure them of your love.

Desired Result: A quick reminder that avoids words of rebuke will bring the students back to order and will make each class member conscious about good behavior.

Items Needed: None

Idea #77: BIBLE VERSE HELP

Situation: *One or two students begin whispering. Others are distracted.*

Solution: Pause in the teaching. Write a Bible verse like Proverbs 1:5: "A wise man will hear, and will increase learning," or Proverbs 4:13: "Take fast hold of instruction; let her not go,"or James 1:19, "...Let every man be swift to hear, slow to speak, and slow to wrath," on the chalkboard and ask the class to repeat it. Then call on a student (preferable one who was not paying attention) and have him/her explain the meaning of the verse. Repeat it together once more. Then continue with the lesson. Each time someone is distracted, ask everyone to repeat the verse again, then ask one who is misbehaving what a particular word means, why God may have put that verse in the Bible, or some other question.

Desired Result: No student is scolded, but every student realizes the importance of listening to the lesson. It is not just because the teacher wants to teach, but because God says to listen to His Word. Children learn to apply the Bible to their actions and think through what it means to them.

Items Needed: Chalkboard and chalk, or paper and pen or marker
Pre-selected Bible verses pertaining to listening and learning

Idea #78: DRESS UP

Situation: *Last week, the students began to fuss. Many said, "I'm bored," and disrupted the other class members.*

Solution: This week, bring extra clothes (like a scarf, vest, blouse or shirt, jacket, hat, gloves, mittens, boots). As you teach the lesson, put on an extra piece of clothing each time the students do what you ask them to do. You will look funny by the end of class, but a good instructor can laugh at himself/herself. If poor behavior develops, take off an added piece of clothing. Bring a camera so a child can take a picture at the end of the class session. Place the picture on the bulletin board with this inscription: "THIS IS WHAT A GOOD CLASS CAN DO TO A TEACHER!"

Desired Result: Willing students behave in an acceptable manner and enjoy the class, building a camaraderie with the teacher.

Items Needed: An extra set of clothing: scarf, vest, shirt, jacket, gloves, hat, mittens, boots, etc.
Polaroid camera loaded with film

Idea #79: FORFEIT THROW

Situation: *After several class sessions, you've discovered that there are several students (or even just one!) who love to act up, to get others to giggle or show off.*

Solution: Bring a beanbag and a large cardboard with two circles on it to class. Make cards with half of them showing a #1 on one side and the other half with #2 on the other side.

The #1 cards could say:
> Stand up and take a bow, then sit in silence.
> Stand up, say, "I want others to learn about Jesus," then sit down.
> Write three times on the chalkboard, "I WANT TO LISTEN."

The #2 cards might say:
> Apologize to the class for causing a problem.
> Place hands over mouth for five minutes.
> Turn chair backward to class and stay that way for three minutes.

Place cardboard on floor and have misbehaving student toss the beanbag onto a circle on the cardboard. Whichever number it is nearest to, he/she should pick a card with a corresponding number and do what it says.

Desired Result: The students learn that misbehavior has consequences.

Items Needed: Beanbag
Large cardboard with a #1 circle and a #2 circle
Two stacks of cards: one with positive actions, the other with reprimanding actions
Timer

Idea #80: NEVER SAY "NO"

Situation: *A student is rebellious, refuses to cooperate, and disrupts the entire class.*

Solution: Pause to play a game. There is only one rule: No one can say "NO." Ask several questions, funny or serious, with "YES" or "NO" answers of several of the students. Then go to the noisy student and ask: "Will you listen?" The student can't say "NO." He/she will have to say "YES." When he/she does, plunge immediately back into the lesson.

Desired Result: The student will realize his/her problem and will probably change his/her behavior for at least a little while.

Items Needed: Prepared list of "yes" or "no" answer questions

Idea #81: BOOK TALK

Situation: *A class needs constant, frequent reminders to pay attention.*

Solution: Make a large book (at least 12" x 18") and print suggestions on each page. Letters must be large (perhaps 3" high and 1/2" thick.) You can use a large black marker or colored marker. Write such words as:

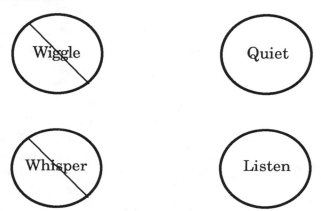

Put each command on a separate page. When the class misbehaves, turn to an appropriate page. You need not speak about the problem, just let the page speak for itself and continue teaching.

You could also make the book a picture book of the desired behavior for those too young to read or to read well.

Desired Result: The silent, visual reminder will most likely make vocal discipline unnecessary. The entire atmosphere of the class will improve.

Items Needed: Several sheets of looseleaf paper
Thick black marker (or colored marker)
Stapler or binder

Idea #82: FLOWERS AND WEEDS

Situation: *Some students will not listen to correction and continue to misbehave on a regular basis.*

Solution: Bring a small window box or carton to class. Fill it with dirt. Bring in some pretty flowers (real, if possible, or silk) and some ugly weeds. Each time a student disobeys or disrupts the class, have the child plant a weed. If a student (any student) is especially cooperative, have him/her plant a flower. No comment need be made after an original explanation of the procedure and the purpose at the beginning of class.

This is also a good object lesson of the types of things we grow in our lives—by planting weeds (sins) or flowers (doing things that honor Christ). Feel free to amplify this idea throughout the lesson with examples students can give. You can make it a class lesson by having students plant a weed for things they list as bad (sin) and flowers for good things.

Desired Result: Students will try to be good and obey the teacher—if only to avoid the weeds. They will view their wrong deeds as weeds and their good deeds as pretty flowers. The teacher will not need to correct the student constantly. The second option makes the discipline less pointed to any particular child and allows each to analyze his/her actions.

Items Needed: Container filled with dirt
Flowers (real or silk)
Weeds
Spade

Idea #83: KEY RING

Situation: *Children (or even one child) try to take over the class with their aggressive behavior.*

Solution: At the beginning of the class period, show the students a key ring with large (six inch) keys on it. Each one has a word printed in letters visible across the classroom. They can say:

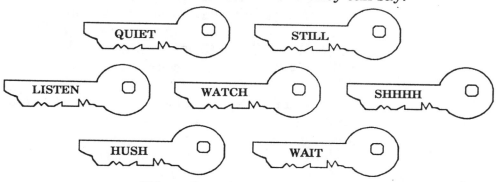

When there is too much noise or the students lack concentration, hold up the keys, find an appropriate one, and pretend to lock your own mouth. The next time, pretend to lock a student's mouth—not necessarily a misbehaving student but one nearby. Another time walk directly to a student who is too loud and pretend to lock his mouth. It will be partially in jest, partially in seriousness. The students will get the message. The teacher can smile and not get upset. The students can quiet down without harsh words, and the lesson can and will go on.

Desired Result: Instead of scolding students for poor behavior, this way shows how unacceptable it is and yet lets all smile and get over the rough time without unpleasantness.

Items Needed: A key ring with oversized (6") keys constructed of cardboard or paper

Idea #84: COUNT HIGH

Situation: *One student is fighting or arguing with another student, keeping not only those two from learning, but also the entire class.*

Solution: If you have noticed an argumentative tendency in your class, explain that you will count when any disturbance starts during class. Explain the scoring of the procedure. If the students stop fighting by number 4, give them an "A"; by 8, give them a "B"; by 10, a "C"; by 15, a "D"; and 20, an "E." Very seldom will you need to count that high.

Then, if a fight or argument arises, say the two students' names and start counting rather than scolding. Probably the two will quiet down, as will the entire class. Your voice can become louder, if necessary, with each number. Praise the students for their self-control, if they stop quickly. Tell them how sad Jesus is with their actions if they take longer. You may also want to follow up by explaining Romans 12:17-21.

Desired Result: The students who are fighting will stop and make a real effort to be disciplined and begin listening...with a game rather than with scolding.

Items Needed: None

Idea #85: RIBBON CUT

Situation: *Some students, in order to show off or to get attention, may, even purposely, destroy a Bible or visuals, spill snacks or paints.*

Solution: Display a 12 inch ribbon and explain that each time someone acts inappropriately, you will cut off an inch of the ribbon. If the ribbon is shorter than six (6) inches at the end of the class period, there will be no game (refreshment, activity, etc.). The students will encourage the misbehaving few to follow through so that the entire class may participate in something special. Be sure to follow through with your promise and take time for a related game, or not have a game if the class does not behave properly.

Desired Result: The class will try hard to improve or avoid their "show off" behavior. The class spirit will help each one work toward cooperation.

Items Needed: 12 inch ribbon
Scissors
Game, refreshment, activity, etc.

Idea #86: BEHAVIOR FOLD

Situation: *Certain students are disrespectful, speaking rudely, raising their voices, interrupting the teacher or other class members.*

Solution: Have a long sheet of paper (approximately 6" x 21"). Fold it every three inches and then unfold it and hang it so all the students can see it. When someone talks out of turn, write, with a thick felt pen, "QUIET." If a particular person doesn't heed the warning, write the student's name ("Joe") under "Quiet." As soon as the admonition is obeyed, fold that suggestion to the back, held by a paper clip. The next time someone acts improperly, print "LISTEN" on the paper. If one or two students don't shape up, write their names under the word, "LISTEN." Fold it back as soon as the class is listening again. Other words to use can be "OBEY," "PLEASE," "STOP TALKING," SIT DOWN." At the end of class, you may want to write, JESUS LOVES...and put each student's name there.

Desired Result: The interesting reminder may be all that it takes to quiet down a class, and there are more folds to remind the class members who forget.

Items Needed: Long sheet of paper (6" x 21")
Thick marker
Paper clips

Idea #87: LIGHTS ON

Situation: *Some students lie—repeatedly—and need help overcoming this sin.*

Solution: Each time a student lies, and it is obvious to you, turn on a flashlight. Ask the student to read I Kings 22:16. Let the student hold the flashlight on the Bible while he/she reads. Ask another student, who was not lying, to explain it. Turn off the light, then go on with the lesson. The class member is very aware of the lie and that the teacher and class members know it. He/she can back off without embarrassment and learn to tell the truth from God's word. If it happens again, use other verses like Psalm 119:30 and use the flashlight again.

Desired Result: The student will get the message without a word spoken and without harsh scolding.

Items Needed: Flashlight
Bible and verses dealing with lying

Idea #88: STRING ALONG

Situation: *Students cannot seem to keep hands to themselves; their actions include hitting, pinching, tickling, pulling hair, etc.*

Solution: Bring a long string—long enough to go around the whole circle of students. When the Bible lesson begins, have each student put both hands on the string and hold them there until the end of that section of the lesson. The teacher can also hold it, except when using a visual. At the end of the lesson, play a game. Place a ring on the string and let the students hide it in their hands, passing it from student to student to see if the teacher can find it. Tell them to move it quickly without being seen.

Desired Result: Students will have hands in check during the Bible lesson and probably will not bother another student. They will also enjoy the concluding game.

Items Needed: A long string or rope
A small ring

Idea #89: MEET DEAC

Situation: *Some students refuse to listen to the teacher.*

Solution: Invite one of the deacons to attend the class and ask him to sit next to the worst student. (Do not identify the student as the "worst" to your visitor.) When introducing the visitor, explain, "He is here to see how well behaved our class is" and give him an opportunity to say a few words. At the end of the class let him congratulate students for good behavior and explain to them that he is a deacon. Ask him to explain what a deacon's job in the church is.

Desired Result: The students will automatically behave better, at least for that one class. They will also prove to themselves what fun a good class can be.

Items Needed: A church deacon

Idea #90: MARK YOURSELF

Situation: *Some students have trouble controlling their tongues. They use swear words, dirty words, mean words, hateful words, or other rude words.*

Solution: At the beginning of class, give students paper and pencils. Ask them to give themselves a mark for how well they think they will control their tongue and act correctly in class. During the class have each class member make notes on what happened in class (Bible lesson, handcraft, game, memory work, etc.). Have them say one thing about the content of each part of the class. (e.g. *Bible lesson*—Studied John 3:16. *Handcraft*—Made bookmark with Bible verse, etc.) At the end of class, let them re-grade themselves and share, if they will, how they accomplished their written goals.

Desired Result: The students will want to guard their tongues and their actions and accomplish what they think they are capable of accomplishing. The process will lead to better tongue control and improved behavior. Taking notes will keep their attention on each part of the class and each one will be able to see what they did and that everyone had the same activities.

Items Needed: Paper and pencils for each student

Idea #91: TAPED SILENCE

Situation: *Some students never want to listen, no matter what the project or section of the class period.*

Solution: Give each student approximately two inches of masking tape. Take one piece yourself. Place the tape over your lips and ask the students to do the same. Teach the lesson for a few minutes via a tape recorder or visuals or by pantomime.

Then take off your tape and point at certain students when you want them to take off their tape. Make it fun, while postponing the tape removal for noisy students (but not allowing them to keep the tape more than another minute). Finally, end that time of the class by saying, "The quiet was beautiful. Let's try to keep our noise level low and pay attention to the lesson without wearing tape next week!"

Desired Result: A quiet class results, probably without any scolding, and without demeaning any student who has trouble with the process of listening.

Items Needed: Masking tape
Prepared visuals or audio/visual tape for teaching

Idea #92: THAT'S GR-R-R-REAT!

Situation: *An overactive child jumps on the table, bangs on the piano, tips over chairs, breaks equipment.*

Solution: Begin the class session by telling a disruptive student, "You're special!" Repeat it every time he/whe does something you are pleased with. Then, when that student does something below class standards, say, "That's not so special." The child will get the message without a scolding (for he probably gets too many). Continue this "You're special" for many weeks. Try to be genuine, pray until you can really love the overactive, poorly-acting student and then you can say it out of godly love.

Desired Result: The student will respond to love and praise and act better. Students flourish on special attention and need it. Behavior will improve drastically.

Items Needed: None

Idea #93: DONUT HOLE PARTY

Situation: *One student hits others, hurting fellow students.*

Solution: Have a time-out chair. If a student hits someone, have the misbehaving student sit in the chair, then go on with the lesson. After five minutes, include the student in the lesson again. At an appropriate time, ask students to help the one who struggles with good behavior to encourage their fellow students and to help him/her not to hurt others. Total class attention on better behavior will probably help everyone, even the disruptor, to be better. After two weeks of "hit-free" behavior, plan a donut hole party. At the end of a teaching session, give thanks and serve donut holes and small glasses of cold milk or hot cocoa from a Thermos.

Desired Result: A happy, contented, listening class, cooperating with each other and the teacher will be the happy result. Students will see how they can help the entire class learn more and how to change their own behavior. They also have some responsibility in total class discipline.

Items Needed: Donut holes
Milk or hot cocoa
—Enough of the above for the whole class

Idea #94: IMPROMPTU BIBLE STUDY

Situation: *The students act silly during the lesson and seem to ignore any attempt at positive classroom management. Or, they may talk disrespectfully, answer questions in an irreverent manner, or raise their voices rudely.*

Solution: Stop the class and explain what you see as the problem. Help them see from God's Word why that behavior is wrong and what God says about it. Some verses you could have the students look up and read are:

Philippians 1:27	I Peter 1:15; 2:12-13
I Timothy 4:12	II Peter 3:11
Hebrews 13:7	Psalm 19:14

Sometimes it is important to stop everything else to deal with serious misbehavior. An impromptu Bible study such as this could make a lasting impression. You might also let the children elect a judge. Each time a student acts in an unacceptable manner, the judge can hear his/her excuses and then prescribe a punishment such as:
- quote a memory verse
- change chairs
- write "I'm sorry" on the chalkboard
- apologize to the teacher and students
- stand behind the circle or table of students
- sit in a certain chair
- step to the back of the room and stand there for 2 minutes

Desired Result: Students will not be upset with the teacher and will want to improve their behavior so they can honor the Lord Jesus Christ. Students can also learn peer responsibility.

Items Needed: Several Bible verses regarding discipline

Idea #95: THE STUDENT IN THE CLASS

Situation: *The class rebels against sitting still while the teacher struggles to teach the lesson.*

Solution: Stop teaching, ask the class to stand. (If the chairs are not already in a circle, place them in a circle for the rest of the teaching session.) Have the children join hands and sing as they walk clockwise around the inside of the chairs:

1) The children in the class,
   The children in the class,
   Hi, ho, they must sit still,
   The children in the class.

2) The children in the class,
   The children in the class,
   Now it's time for Sunday School,
   The children must sit still.

Each one must sit right where they are standing at the end of the song. The teacher continues the lesson.

Desired Result: A break, movement, smiles, correction without anger, and an opportunity to get back to a lesson that can be taught without struggle.

Items Needed: None

Idea #96: FLOOR TILE FUN

Situation: *Some children are in the habit of calling other students names which are hurtful.*

Solution: Place a linoleum floor tile in front of the class. With a permanent marker, write, "Let the words of my mouth...be acceptable in thy sight, O Lord..." (Psalm 19:14). Pass the tile around the room and ask each student to sign it, indicating their willingness to watch their words, the name calling, everything that comes from their lips. Hang the tile on the wall in front of the class. Once in a while, draw attention to it. If the remarks continue, write on a second tile, "...Let us love one another: for love is of God..." (I John 4:7). Other verses you could use are I John 4:11; I Corinthians 13:4-5; Romans 12:10 or 13:10.

Desired Result: Students will prefer to have nice words come from their mouths because they have heard and signed their names to a Bible verse about what God expects to hear from their lips. Most will change their words to honor Christ.

Items Needed: A linoleum floor tile
A thick permanent marker
Heavy tape

Idea #97: SORRY, SORRY

Situation: *One or two students are ruining the class time for all the students. They distract the teacher. They make noises so others can't hear; they pester everyone sitting near them.*

Solution: At the beginning of class, tell the students that you have something special for them. Do not call any names, but announce to the class that they will be playing a game during the lesson. The game is called: "Sorry, Sorry." Practice it once. Point to any student (the first time let it be a good student) and say their first name. That child must stand, take a bow and say, "Sorry, Sorry." At any time during the session, when you point to a student, that student must stand, bow, and say, "Sorry, Sorry." When a student begins to act in an unacceptable manner, point to him or her immediately. Do not scold the student, just make him do what is required. Keep at it throughout the entire class session.

Desired Result: Students will want to behave after several bow at the teacher's pointed finger.

Items Needed: None

Idea #98: PIANO CHORDS

Situation: *A few class members are negative to every suggestion. They destroy the willingness of the majority of students to learn. Whether it is memory work, lesson time, discussions, or crafts, their first reaction is, "I don't want to do that."*

Solution: Select a few of the class "rules." Show the class that different piano chords will mean different things: A low chord of C–E–G can mean "I will cooperate." An octave higher of the C–E–G chord could mean, "I will enjoy this part of Sunday School." And a still higher C–E–G chord (two octaves above middle C) could mean "Jesus is listening."

Always use the same chord for the same phrase. After a couple of times, the students know without being told.

Desired Result: A class will realize, without harsh words, that being negative harms the whole class. They will do what is suggested without reprimand and a happier atmosphere will prevail. The musical application to the rules will make them a little more enjoyable and a little more memorable.

Items Needed: A musical instrument (if there is no piano in the room, bring a guitar, flute, clarinet, recorder, handbells, etc.)

Idea #99: POPSICLE STICK DROP

Situation: *Some students repeatedly come with the idea of misbehaving, trying the teacher's patience, and being disruptive. Some students throw pencils, papers, chalk, or other classroom materials.*

Solution: Begin the session with a game called "POPSICLE STICK DROP." Print on popsicle or craft sticks, with a fine marker, several suggestions for a happy class hour like, "I will listen"; "I will cooperate"; "I will behave"; "I will learn my lesson"; "I will respect the other students"; "I will respect my teacher." Also, write a value on the sticks: 100 points, 200 points, 300 points. Place a wide-mouthed jar on the floor. Each student chooses three popsicle sticks from a stack, reads the suggestion and the number of points, then tries to drop each stick (from waist level) into the jar. Keep score and allow each student to have two turns. If the class is large, provide two jars and have two teams. After the game, have the one with the highest score choose a different chair than before. Then go down the scores until everyone is back in a chair, everyone in a different place and better able to listen to the Bible lesson.

Desired Result: The game allows students to learn what is expected of them, yet it is not a direct accusation against any child. Each learns the discipline lesson and should try to behave correctly. The game serves as an opportunity to get away from the lesson long enough to stretch muscles and relax attitudes. The new seating arrangement will automatically make for better discipline.

Items Needed: A wide-mouthed jar
Pre-marked popsicle (or craft) sticks, three for each child

Idea #100: PUZZLE PARTS

Situation: *Some students cheat on games and quizzes.*

Solution: Put together an old children's puzzle with large pieces. On the back side, print words that will remind the class about cheating. Such as:

"GOD'S WAY IS THE BEST WAY."

"FOR TO ME TO LIVE IS CHRIST...." (Philippians 1:21)

"AND WHATSOEVER YE DO IN WORD OR DEED, DO ALL IN THE NAME OF THE LORD JESUS."
(Colossians 3:17)

"CHEATING DOESN'T PLEASE GOD."

"HONESTY PLEASES GOD."

"I WANT TO HONOR THE LORD."

"CHEATING HURTS ME."

"GOD SEES MY HEART."

If this is a recurring problem, plan a class where the students put it together and can discuss it as they read the correct behavior. God knows hearts, and He will speak to the students.

Desired Result: Cheaters will realize the teacher *and* God know what they are doing without scolding or anger. Let God do the convicting!

Items Needed: An old children's puzzle with encouragement and helpful phrases printed on the back of each piece

Idea #101: PIN DROP

Situation: *The class is naughty; order has disappeared. You must have their attention so the lesson can be taught.*

Solution: Announce that there must be quiet. Hold a large safety pin (heavy and easier to hear) in your hand as high as possible. As soon as there is some silence, drop the pin. Ask the students who can hear it to raise their hands. If there are a few who didn't hear the pin drop, pick it up and try again. Do it until it is quiet enough for all of the children to hear the pin drop. Explain quietly that their actions were not pleasing to either you or the Lord and that when it is quiet enough to hear a pin drop, it is quiet enough to learn God's Word. Then, immediately go back to teaching.

Desired Result: The students quiet down in a non-threatening atmosphere and all of the class is silent at the same time —group spirit! Teaching may continue.

Items Needed: One large safety pin

Conclusion

There we have it, *101 Creative Discipline Ideas* for those times WHEN KIDS BEND THE RULES. Good discipline can be fun for both the teacher and the class. Everyone is happier when the class works together to learn and listen and hear God's Word. Positive discipline is good classroom management.

Poor discipline is a symptom. It's up to you to discover the problem. The classroom could have a poor physical arrangement such as inadequate ventilation; it could be too crowded, or have too many distractions. Children could have serious home problems or actual learning disabilities. Be sensitive to things you can do to love each child and to correct any negative attitudes or circumstances.

Never select one discipline method and use it constantly, either. It will work a time or two, but then it will fizzle. Rather, use this book to come up with fresh ideas week after week. Eventually, a well-disciplined class won't need these ideas at all.

As you help students to realize that they are in God's house to study God's Word, bear in mind that the children before you were placed there by God. If anyone is allowed to act up or disturb the class, they cheat you and the other children. Be committed to doing whatever is necessary to maintain a positive, disciplined learning environment where the truths of God's Word can be heard and understood.

As the result of good discipline, regular prayer for each child, and students who are really listening, you will see changed lives—students coming to faith in Jesus Christ and seeking to serve Him with their actions, their hearts, and their minds.

The prayer of this author is for the souls of boys and girls to be won to Jesus Christ while they are still young, to learn to live disciplined lives, and to take that characteristic with them throughout a lifetime of dedication to their Saviour. May God bless each of you.